BatterUp Kids dELiCiOuS DeSSerTs

Sweet Treats from the Premier Children's Cooking School

BARBARA BEERY

Photography by Marty Snortum

GIBBS SMITH

Gibbs Smith, Publisher
Salt Lake City

First Edition
08 07 06 05 04   5 4 3 2 1

Published by
Gibbs Smith, Publisher
P.O. Box 667
Layton, Utah 84041

Orders: 1.800.748.5439
www.gibbs-smith.com

Designed by Dawn DeVries Sokol
Food styling by Harriet Granthen
Printed and bound in Hong Kong

To all the children who have taken classes at Batter Up Kids Cooking School

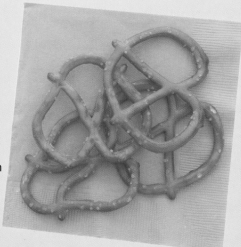

Disclaimer: Children should always have adult supervision when working in the kitchen. The publisher and author assume no responsibility for any damages or injuries incurred while making any of the recipes in this book.

Library of Congress Cataloging-in-Publication Data

Beery, Barbara, 1954–
Batter up kids : delicious desserts / Barbara Beery ; photographs by Marty Snortum.— 1st ed.
    p. cm.
  ISBN 1-58685-365-1
  1. Desserts—Juvenile literature. I. Snortum, Marty. II. Title.
TX773 .B417 2004   641.8'6—dc22

                                    2003021029

CONTENTS

NOW WE'RE COOKING!

1. Get ready! Push your sleeves back, tie on your apron, wash your hands, and make sure your work area is clean and spotless.

2. Now get all of the bowls, utensils, and ingredients you will need for the recipe you are going to make. Place them in your work area and make sure you have everything ready.

3. Ask a grown-up to be your chef's assistant.

4. Now it's Recipe Time! Read through the recipe with your assistant and make sure you both understand what to do.

5. Remember, it is much easier to clean up as you go. Fill a big sink or washtub full of warm, soapy water and get a sponge or washcloth. Wipe up as you go. Put each dish and utensil into the sink after you've finished with it. When your recipe is made, you'll almost have everything cleaned up, too. Easy as pie!

6. Don't forget to thank your grown-up assistant for helping you. Do you know the best way to say thanks? Offer them the first bite of your delicious dessert. With a reward like that, they'll want to help you every time!

KITCHEN SAFETY PATROL

Keep these rules in mind to help you use the oven, stovetop, and microwave correctly and safely. Always ask a grown-up to be in the kitchen when you are going to use the oven or stovetop.

Hot Potato! (The Oven)

PREHEAT BEFORE BAKING ANYTHING. "Preheating" means to bring your oven to the temperature it calls for in a recipe. This usually takes about 10 minutes. It is important to let the oven get to the correct temperature for the recipe you're making *before* you put the dish in the oven. Why? As the oven heats up, it puts out extra heat to catch up to the temperature it's supposed to be (350 degrees, for example). The oven temperature will burn—not bake—your food if you put it in while the oven preheats.

DON'T OPEN AND PEEK! When you open the oven door, heat escapes, so it will take longer for your dish to bake. Turn on the inside oven light to peek instead.

USE HOT PADS OR OVEN MITTS when taking items from the oven. Have someone help you if you don't feel comfortable removing hot items from the oven yourself.

Where There's Smoke There's Fire! (The Stovetop)

KEEP THE HANDLES of the cooking pans from hanging over the edge of the stove. This keeps you safe from bumping into a handle and spilling the hot liquid on you.

LIGHTLY TOUCH THE TOP OF A LID on your cook pot to test if you can remove it safely without a hot pad. If it's too hot, then use a hot pad or ask your grown-up assistant to help.

OPEN THE LID of a saucepan or pot away from you. This protects your face and hands from the hot steam.

Zappin' It! (The Microwave)

ALWAYS ASK A GROWN-UP if the dish or bowl you want to use is "microwave-safe." Some dishes even have "microwave-safe" printed on them. *Never* put foil or anything metal in the microwave.

REMEMBER, when you use a microwave, the ingredients inside a dish will be very hot, just like when they come out of an oven.

REMOVE CAREFULLY, and make sure the container is cool to the touch before you pull it out of the microwave. Sometimes even microwave-safe dishes and bowls have a "hot spot" on one side while the other side remains cool.

APES FOR CREPES

Makes 12 to 15 (8-inch) crepes

FOR CREPES:

4 eggs

1 cup milk

½ teaspoon salt

1 cup flour

1 tablespoon butter, melted (do not use margarine or soft-spread margarine)

1 teaspoon vanilla

To make batter for crepes:

Beat eggs and milk with a whisk or fork in a medium-sized mixing bowl. Add flour and salt, and mix until very smooth.

Add butter and vanilla. Blend well.

Put mixture in refrigerator for 30 minutes (it will thicken up).

🍳 APES FOR CREPES 🍳

FOR FILLING:

1 to 2 scoops of ice cream or frozen yogurt for each crepe (your favorite flavor)

Any fresh fruits (strawberries, raspberries, bananas, peaches, pineapple), cut into bite-size pieces

To prepare crepes:

Spray a nonstick skillet lightly with nonstick cooking spray. Preheat skillet over medium heat on stovetop.

With a ladle or large spoon, pour about 2 tablespoons of batter into the center of the heated skillet. Tilt and turn it until the batter covers the entire bottom of the skillet. Cook for about 30 seconds or until lightly browned.

Using a spatula, flip the crepe over and cook 10 to 15 seconds more.

Slide cooked crepe out of skillet and cool on waxed paper or foil. Continue making crepes until all the batter is used.

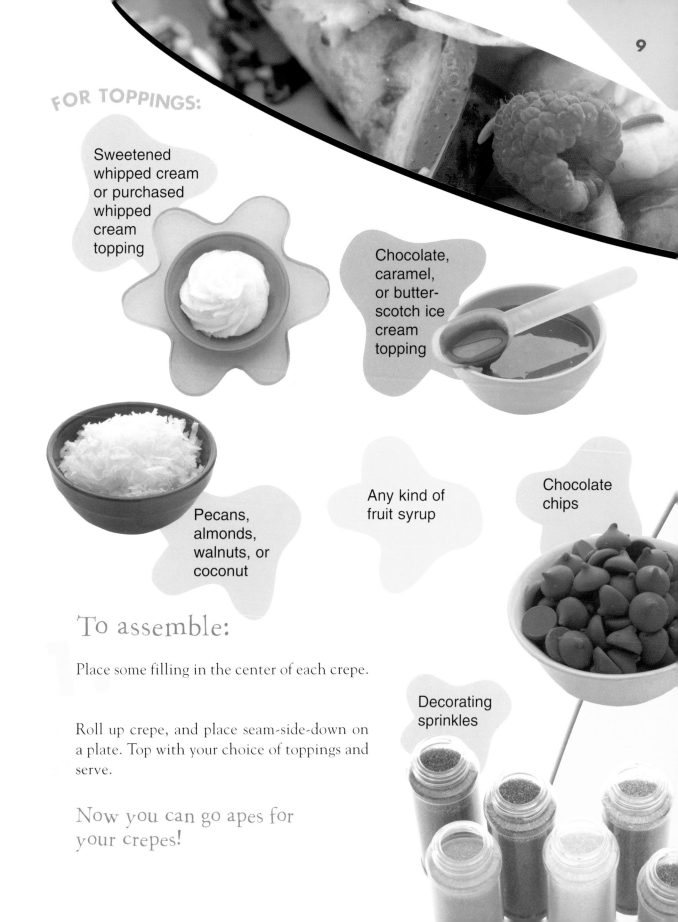

FOR TOPPINGS:

Sweetened whipped cream or purchased whipped cream topping

Chocolate, caramel, or butter-scotch ice cream topping

Pecans, almonds, walnuts, or coconut

Any kind of fruit syrup

Chocolate chips

Decorating sprinkles

To assemble:

Place some filling in the center of each crepe.

Roll up crepe, and place seam-side-down on a plate. Top with your choice of toppings and serve.

Now you can go apes for your crepes!

CANDY-COATED DRAGONFLIES

Makes 8 dragonflies

8 to 10 squares vanilla candy coating or vanilla almond bark

Food coloring, optional

8 (8-inch) pretzel rods

16 large pretzel twists

Assorted decorating sugars or sprinkles

1. Melt candy coating according to package directions. Remove from heat and pour into 2 or 3 small bowls. You may add 2 to 4 drops of food coloring to each bowl. Stir to blend color.

2. Place pretzel rods on foil-lined cookie sheet sprayed with nonstick cooking spray (about 3 inches apart from each other). These are the dragonflies' long bodies.

3. Carefully spoon the warm melted candy coating over each pretzel rod to cover completely.

4. Dip each pretzel twist in the candy coating and place one on each side of the upper half of the pretzel rod. The pretzel twists should actually rest on top of the pretzel rod and just barely touch one another. This forms the dragonfly's wings.

5. Sprinkle each dragonfly pretzel with colored sugars or sprinkles.

6. Place cookie sheet in freezer for 5 to 10 minutes to allow candy coating to harden.

7. Remove from freezer and carefully take each dragonfly off cookie sheet to serve.

Don't let them fly away before you have a chance to take a bite!

CHOCOLATE-COVERED UNICORN HORNS

Makes 10 to 12 unicorn horns

8 to 10 squares chocolate candy coating or chocolate almond bark

10 to 12 waffle or wafer-type ice cream cones with pointed ends

Assorted decorating sprinkles placed in small dishes or bowls

1 small package mini marsh-mallows

Sliced fresh fruits (strawberries, bananas, peaches, and so on)

1. Melt chocolate candy coating or chocolate almond bark according to package directions.

2. Place melted chocolate in a medium-sized bowl. Dip about 1½ to 2 inches of each cone (the big, open end) into melted chocolate.

3. Now take each chocolate dipped "unicorn horn" and dip the chocolate-covered end into decorating sprinkles.

4. Place each finished unicorn horn carefully on a foil-lined cookie sheet sprayed with non-stick cooking spray. Place in freezer 5 to 10 minutes to harden chocolate.

5. Remove from freezer. Fill each unicorn horn with mini marshmallows and sliced fresh fruits to serve.

These unicorn horns are so good you'll think it's magic!

FLYING FROG PUDDING

Makes 6 servings

2½ cups cold whole or 2% milk (whole milk works best)

2 (1-gallon) plastic zipper-lock bags

Green food coloring

1 large package (5.9 ounces) Jell-O brand instant vanilla pudding

6 lettuce leaves (to make lily pads)

Fresh flowers for garnish*

Measure cold milk into a pitcher and add 3 to 5 drops of green food coloring.

Place contents of instant vanilla pudding into one of the plastic bags.

Add green milk to pudding in bag.

Securely close bag. Place first plastic bag inside second plastic bag and securely close the second bag.

Now get ready for the fun! Get your friends and form a circle, standing about 5 feet away from each other. Throw the bag back and forth and watch your frog pudding fly through the air for about 5 minutes. When 5 minutes are up, chill pudding in the refrigerator for 4 minutes.

While you wait for the pudding to chill, get 6 serving plates and put one lettuce leaf on each plate. Then remove the pudding from the refrigerator. Remove the inner plastic bag from the outer plastic bag. With the help of your adult assistant, snip off one corner of the plastic bag with a pair of scissors and squeeze out a portion of the pudding on top of each "lily pad" lettuce leaf. Garnish with a fresh flower.

Hop on over to the table and enjoy!

*Be sure to use flowers that are non-poisonous and pesticide-free.

LADYBUGS ON A STICK

Makes 12 ladybugs

1. Place a grape on a wooden skewer or tooth-pick, sliding it all the way to the end of the stick. This is the ladybug's head.

2. Next place a strawberry on the skewer, stem end first, and slide it down to touch the grape. This is the ladybug's body.

3. Lay the ladybug down and carefully push the pointed ends of several chocolate chips into the strawberry to make the ladybug's spots.

Now you have a ladybug on a stick!

12 seedless red or green grapes

12 whole strawberries with stems

12 (6- to 8-inch) wooden skewers or colored toothpicks

1 package mini-morsel chocolate chips

IGLOO ICE POPS

Makes 12 to 15 ice pops

1½ to 2 cups fresh or frozen raspberries, blueberries, sliced kiwi, or strawberries

Combine all ingredients except powdered sugar in a large bowl. Stir carefully, trying to keep the berries whole.

Divide fruit mixture evenly between Popsicle molds or small paper cups. If using paper cups, cover each cup with a foil square. Poke a hole in the foil and insert a wooden Popsicle stick or the straight end of a plastic spoon.

Place ice pops on a cookie sheet and freeze for 3 to 4 hours.

Chef's Secret: For a cool way to serve these pops, sprinkle with "snowflakes" of powdered sugar.

Chill out with your igloo ice pops!

1 cup apple juice or cranapple juice

A tiny pinch of salt

3 to 5 tablespoons granulated sugar (to taste)

Powdered sugar (optional)

CRISPY CREAMY ICE CREAM SANDWICHES

Makes 12 ice cream sandwiches

1. Spray a medium saucepan with nonstick cooking spray. Melt butter or margarine with marshmallows in pan, stirring often. Stir in vanilla. Add cereal and remove from heat.

2. Stir together until a large ball begins to form. Add candies or sprinkles, if desired.

3. Scoop mix into a 9 x 13-inch pan sprayed with nonstick cooking spray. Flatten, then chill in the refrigerator for 10 minutes. Remove from refrigerator and cut into 2-inch squares.

4. Put a small scoop of ice cream on top of one square and top with another square. Trim off extra ice cream so it is square. Press together and eat right away, or place in freezer until ready to serve.

Voilà! Ice cream sandwiches!

¼ cup (½ stick) butter or margarine (do not use soft-spread margarine)

1 (10-ounce) bag marsh-mallows

1 teaspoon vanilla

6 cups crispy rice cereal

½ cup decorating sprinkles or multicolored coated chocolate candies (optional)

Ice cream, sorbet, or frozen yogurt

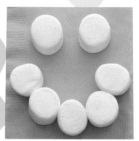

FLOWERPOT ICE CREAM

Makes 4 servings

4 (3-inch) clay flowerpots

4 cookies or 4 small pieces of cake

Ice cream, sorbet, or frozen yogurt (your favorite flavor)

2 drinking straws, cut in half

Chocolate syrup

Assorted decorating sprinkles

4 fresh or silk flowers

1. Wash and dry new clay pots.

2. Place cookies or pieces of cake in the bottom of each clay pot. Press down, making sure they cover the hole in the bottom of each pot.

3. Put a scoop of ice cream into each flowerpot and drizzle with chocolate syrup. Decorate with sprinkles.

4. Insert a straw into the scoop of ice cream. Place the flower stem inside the straw.

5. Place each Flowerpot Ice Cream on a small saucer and serve. Flowerpot Ice Cream may be covered and stored in the freezer before inserting flowers into straws.

It's flower power fun!

MOUNTAINS OF MUD PIES

Makes 6 to 8 servings

1 pint each: vanilla ice cream, caramel ice cream, and chocolate ice cream

Whipped cream topping

7 to 8 whole graham crackers, OR 20 to 25 gingersnaps, OR 15 to 20 chocolate-cream sandwich cookies

Fudge ice cream topping

½ cup chopped pecans, almonds, or walnuts (optional)

2 (1-gallon) plastic zipper-lock bags

Take ice cream out of freezer to soften.

Place graham crackers or cookies in a zipper-lock bag. Close bag, then place it in a second zipper-lock bag. Secure tightly.

Crush graham crackers or cookies with a rolling pin or rubber mallet.

4 tablespoons butter or margarine, melted

MOUNTAINS OF MUD PIES

Empty crumbs into a medium-sized bowl, and stir in melted butter or margarine.

Press an equal amount of crumbs in each of 4 mini pie pans, or press all of the crumbs into one 9-inch pie pan.

Chill in freezer for about 15 minutes. Remove from freezer.

Scoop the softened vanilla ice cream into pans first. Top with the caramel ice cream, then top with the chocolate ice cream. Make sure to smooth the ice cream between each layer. This is your "mud."

Top it off with whipped cream and a drizzle of fudge ice cream topping.

Sprinkle with chopped nuts, if you like. These are your "pebbles."

Chill mud pies in freezer 1 hour or longer before serving.

Take a bite of your mountain-high mud pie!

BAKED SNOWBALLS

Makes 4 to 6 snowballs

1. Preheat oven to 500 degrees.

2. Use 2-inch or 3-inch round baking dishes or ramekins. Square dishes will not work. Cut each slice of cake into a circle so that it fits into the bottom of the baking dish. Place a circle of cake on the bottom of each dish.

3. Now fill the dishes to the top with ice cream, frozen yogurt, or sorbet. Then place filled dishes on a cookie sheet and put in freezer.

4 to 6 slices of cake

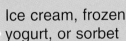

Ice cream, frozen yogurt, or sorbet

BAKED SNOWBALLS

3 egg whites, room temperature

¼ teaspoon cream of tartar

4 tablespoons sugar

½ teaspoon vanilla

Chocolate syrup (for garnish)

Maraschino cherries (for garnish)

4. Place egg whites in a mixing bowl and whip until frothy (like soapsuds).

5. Add cream of tartar and beat until soft peaks form (like shaving cream).

6. Gradually add sugar and then vanilla. Continue to beat until smooth and shiny (another 2 to 3 minutes).

7. Remove ice cream–filled dishes from freezer and spread the snow meringue over the top of each of the ice cream cups. Make very sure the snow forms a "blanket" over the ice cream. There should be absolutely NO ice cream showing.

8. Put snowballs on cookie sheet and place in oven. Bake until golden brown, from 1 to 3 minutes. Watch very closely, as they brown quickly.

9. Take snowballs out of the oven and garnish each with chocolate syrup and a cherry. Serve immediately.

These snowballs are too good to throw!

ANGEL PUFFS

Makes 24 puffs

1 package angel
food cake mix

1 teaspoon
vanilla
extract

½ teaspoon
almond
extract

¼ cup
confetti
nonpareils

Preheat oven to 350 degrees.

Make cake mix according to package directions, adding vanilla and almond extracts.

Mix on low speed for about 1 minute, then mix on medium for 1 more minute.

Fold in nonpareils.

Line 2 (12-cup) muffin pans with foil muffin cup liners. Spoon batter into each muffin cup, filling ¾ full. Bake about 25 minutes, or until the top is dark golden brown. Do not underbake.

Carefully remove puffs from oven and cool in pan 5 minutes. Take puffs out of muffin pans and cool at least 1 hour before frosting.

Frost with "clouds" of whipped cream on each puff and sprinkle with coconut.

These taste heavenly!

2 to 3 cups
whipped cream
or whipped
cream topping

1 cup
flaked
coconut

HIDDEN TREASURE KING'S CAKE

Makes 1 (12-inch) cake

1 package large or "grand" size biscuits

¼ cup (½ stick) butter, melted

¼ cup granulated sugar mixed with 1 tablespoon cinnamon

Coins, tiny plastic dolls, or any kind of trinket out of a vending machine that won't melt when baked.*

Decorating sugars (yellow, purple, and green)

Preheat oven to 350 degrees.

Place biscuits on a lightly floured work area and roll them together into a large circle. Brush with melted butter and sprinkle with cinnamon-sugar mixture.

Place 3 to 5 hidden treasures anywhere on the dough.

Beginning at the side closest to you, roll up dough into a cylinder. Put seam-side-down on a cookie sheet lined with foil and sprayed with nonstick cooking spray.

Form dough into a ring and pinch the ends together tightly so they don't come apart when baking.

Bake for 30 to 40 minutes or until lightly browned.

Remove from oven. Using a pastry brush, brush lightly with 1 tablespoon water and sprinkle generously with colored sugars.

Slice and serve warm. Remember to be careful with each bite . . . you might find a treasure!

It's time to go treasure hunting!

*Warn your guests about the hidden treasures so they don't swallow them!

PINK PRINCESS CAKE

Makes 1 round 2-layer cake

To make cake:

1. Preheat oven to 350 degrees.

2. In a medium-sized bowl, cream together butter and sugar with an electric mixer. Beat in eggs, one at a time. Then stir in vanilla.

3. Stir a small amount of pink food dye into the milk and set aside. In another bowl, combine flour, baking powder, and salt. Add to batter alternately with colored milk. Beat until smooth and creamy, about 1 minute.

4. Pour batter into 1 (8-inch) round cake pan and 1 (6-inch) round cake pan, each sprayed generously with nonstick cooking spray and lined with circles of waxed paper or parchment paper.

½ cup butter, softened

1 cup sugar

2 eggs

2 teaspoons vanilla

Pink gel-type food dye

2 teaspoons baking powder

½ cup milk

¼ teaspoon salt

1½ cups flour

PINK PRINCESS CAKE

FOR FROSTING:

¼ cup butter, softened

4 cups powdered sugar

1 teaspoon vanilla

Pink gel-type food dye

2 tablespoons milk (more if frosting is too stiff)

Confetti sprinkles

5. Bake 30 to 35 minutes. The smaller cake may be done a few minutes before the bigger cake. Cakes should be golden brown. When touched lightly, it should not leave a fingerprint.

6. Cool in pans 10 to 15 minutes, then carefully remove by placing a plate or rack over each cake pan and inverting the cake onto the plate or rack. Cool another 10 to 15 minutes before frosting.

7. When cakes are cool, center smaller cake on top of larger one.

To make frosting:

1. Beat butter in a large bowl with an electric mixer. Slowly add powdered sugar, ½ cup at a time, alternately with milk. Add vanilla.

2. Stir in a tiny bit of pink gel food coloring. Add extra milk, 1 tablespoon at a time, if necessary.

3. Frost and decorate with sprinkles.

A cake fit for a princess!

YOU ARE MY SUNSHINE CUPCAKES

Makes 24 cupcakes

YOU ARE MY SUNSHINE CUPCAKES

FOR CAKE:

1 box yellow cake mix

Apple or pineapple juice

FOR FROSTING:

1 can vanilla frosting

½ cup powdered sugar

½ teaspoon vanilla

Yellow and red food coloring

To make cupcakes:

1. Preheat oven to 350 degrees.

2. Prepare cake mix according to package directions, substituting apple or pineapple juice for the water.

3. Line 2 (12-cup) muffin pans with paper liners.

Fill each cup ¾ full of batter. Bake 20 to 25 minutes at 350 degrees. Remove from oven and cool in pan 5 minutes.

Take cupcakes out of pan and cool 10 to 15 minutes before frosting.

1 small bag of matchstick-sized pretzel sticks

To make Sunshine frosting:

Mix canned frosting, powdered sugar, vanilla, 8 drops yellow food coloring, and 5 drops red food coloring in a large bowl. Blend well.

Frost cupcakes.

1 package mini-sized M&M's

Tubes of decorating gels (optional)

To decorate:

At the very top sides of the cupcakes, insert 7 to 9 pretzel sticks going around in a circle. This makes the "rays" of sunshine.

Use M&M's and optional decorating gels for the eyes, nose, and mouth.

Bring a little "sunshine" to someone you love!

VOLCANO CUPCAKES
WITH BUTTERCREAM LAVA

Makes 24 cupcakes

FOR CUPCAKES:

1 package Red Velvet cake mix or Devil's Food cake mix

24 Hershey's Kisses, unwrapped

To make cupcakes:

Preheat oven to 350 degrees.

Make cake mix according to package directions.

Spray 2 (12-cup) muffin pans generously with nonstick cooking spray. Pour batter into muffin cups, filling each cup ¾ full.

Bake for 20 to 25 minutes, until the tops of cupcakes spring back when gently touched. Carefully remove pans from oven.

Push 1 Hershey's Kiss into the center of each warm cupcake, making a "crater."

Remove cupcakes from pan. Cool at least 20 minutes before frosting.

VOLCANO CUPCAKES

WITH BUTTERCREAM LAVA

FOR FROSTING:

½ cup (1 stick) butter, room temperature

4 cups powdered sugar

1½ teaspoons vanilla

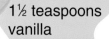

1 to 3 tablespoons milk

Yellow and red food coloring

Red decorating sprinkles (optional)

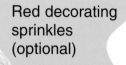

To make Buttercream Lava frosting:

With an electric mixer, beat butter in a large bowl.

Add powdered sugar, ½ cup at a time, until you have used all 4 cups.

Add vanilla and 1 tablespoon milk. Mix until smooth and creamy. Put 5 drops of red and 2 drops of yellow food coloring into frosting. Stir to blend. If frosting is too thick, add rest of the milk, 1 tablespoon at a time.

Frost cupcakes generously with piles of buttercream lava, letting some drip down the sides.

Top with fire red sprinkles, if you like.

It's an explosion of good tastes!

JUMPING FOR GINGERBREAD COOKIES

Makes 24 (2-inch) cookies

JUMPING FOR GINGERBREAD COOKIES

FOR COOKIES:

¾ cup butter, softened

½ teaspoon cloves

½ teaspoon nutmeg

½ cup brown sugar, packed

2 teaspoons ginger

1 teaspoon cinnamon

1 egg

3 cups flour

¼ teaspoon salt

¾ cup molasses

Powdered sugar for rolling out dough

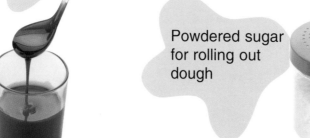

1. Preheat oven to 350 degrees.

2. In a large bowl, combine butter, brown sugar, egg, and molasses.

3. Stir in dry ingredients and mix completely. Cover bowl and put in refrigerator for 2 to 3 hours.

4. Take out small portions, about ¼ cup or ½ cup, of the cookie dough, and roll out to ¼- to ½-inch thickness. Use powdered sugar instead of flour to roll out cookie dough. It won't toughen cookies as flour does if too much is used.

5. Bake on a foil-lined cookie sheet sprayed with nonstick cooking spray for 8 to 12 minutes, depending on size of cookie.

6. Make frosting using recipe for Decorator frosting on page 52.

7. Let cookies cool on cookie sheet for 5 minutes, then carefully remove. Cool another 10 minutes before frosting and decorating.

You'll jump for joy with every bite!

FOR FROSTING:

Use recipe for Decorator frosting on page 52

FOR DECORATING:

Assorted candies and decorating sprinkles

FANCY FORTUNE COOKIES

Makes 12 fortune cookies

1 package refrigerated piecrusts

2 to 3 tablespoons cornstarch sprinkled on work area

1 tablespoon water

Colored decorating sugars, each one in a small saucer

Preheat oven to 350 degrees.

Write a note of good fortune or draw little symbols (a sun, moon, heart, or flower) on two-inch-long pieces of paper with a pen or nontoxic marker.

Sprinkle cornstarch on your work area and smooth it with your hand.

Unfold 1 piecrust at a time and place on work area. Turn over crust to dust both sides with cornstarch. Flatten and smooth out wrinkles with rolling pin. With a 3-inch-round cookie cutter, cut out 4 to 6 circles per piecrust. You may re-roll scraps if you wish.

Put 1 fortune in the center of each circle and fold in half. Then fold the semicircle in half.

Brush each fortune cookie with a little water to moisten. Dip one side of each cookie into a colored sugar then place on cookie sheet, sugar-side-up. Place cookies 2 inches apart.

Bake for 15 to 20 minutes or until lightly browned.

Carefully take from oven and cool 5 minutes before removing from pan.

Good fortune is coming your way!

A SKILLET FULL OF COOKIES

Makes 1 giant cookie, 16 slices

½ cup white sugar

1 cup brown sugar, packed

1 cup (2 sticks) butter, softened

1 teaspoon vanilla

2 eggs

1 teaspoon baking soda

2½ cups flour

1 teaspoon salt

2 cups milk chocolate chips

1. Preheat oven to 375 degrees.

2. In a large bowl, use a mixer to cream together the sugars and the butter until smooth. Beat in vanilla and add eggs, one at a time.

3. Add the flour, baking soda, and salt. Mix well. Dough will be stiff.

4. Using a large spoon, stir in the chocolate chips.

5. Spray a 10-inch skillet (with an ovenproof metal or wooden handle) with nonstick cooking spray. Pat cookie dough into skillet and bake approximately 30 minutes or until the edges are lightly browned.

6. Cool for 15 minutes, then slice.

Take a bite out of this!

THUMBS-UP COOKIES

Makes 24 cookies

¾ cup shortening

1. Preheat oven to 350 degrees.

2. Line a cookie sheet with foil. Spray with nonstick cooking spray.

3. In a large mixing bowl, cream the shortening and sugar. Blend in peanut butter, salt, egg, vanilla, and flour. Mix well.

4. Shape dough into 1-inch balls. Press your thumb into the center of each ball, creating a ½-inch indented spot.

5. Bake for 12 to 15 minutes and cool on a rack. Fill centers with your favorite jelly or jam.

Give yourself a big thumbs-up!

½ cup brown sugar, packed

½ cup peanut butter

½ teaspoon salt

1 teaspoon vanilla

1 egg

1¾ cups flour

Jelly or jam

TOTALLY TEA CAKE COOKIES

FOR COOKIES:

Makes 36 cookies

To make cookies:

1. Preheat oven to 375 degrees.

2. Cream butter in a large mixing bowl. Add sugar, beating until light and fluffy. Add egg and vanilla, mixing well.

3. Combine flour, baking soda, and salt in a separate bowl. Add to creamed mixture, blending well. Dough will be very stiff.

4. Divide dough into thirds. Roll each portion to ⅛-inch thickness on lightly floured work area. Cut with assorted cookie cutters. Place cookies 2 inches apart on cookie sheets sprayed with nonstick cooking spray.

½ cup (1 stick) butter or margarine, softened

¾ cup sugar

1 egg

¾ teaspoon vanilla

½ teaspoon baking soda

2 cups flour

½ teaspoon salt

TOTALLY TEA CAKE COOKIES

FOR FROSTING:

3 tablespoons commercial meringue powder

2 cups powdered sugar

¼ cup plus 2 tablespoons warm water

½ teaspoon almond extract

Food coloring

1 teaspoon vanilla

Decorating sugars

5 Bake for 8 to 10 minutes or until lightly browned. Remove to wire racks to cool. Frost and decorate as desired.

To make Decorator frosting:

Combine meringue powder, powdered sugar, water, and vanilla and almond extracts in a mixing bowl.

Beat on high speed with an electric mixer for 3 to 5 minutes.

Divide in separate bowls and add drops of food color as desired.

Make these for your next tea party!

STACK 'EM HIGH
STRAWBERRY
SHORTCAKES

Makes 4 to 5 servings

STACK 'EM HIGH STRAWBERRY SHORTCAKES

FOR SHORTCAKES:

1 package frozen puff pastry dough

¼ cup butter, melted

2 tablespoons granulated sugar

To make shortcakes:

Thaw dough for 30 minutes before using.

Preheat oven to 375 degrees.

Open 1 sheet of puff pastry and place on floured work area. Gently roll out and smooth pastry.

Use a star-shaped or round cookie cutter to cut out a total of 12 to 15 shaped pastries.

Place individual pastries on a foil-lined cookie sheet sprayed with nonstick cooking spray. Brush pastries lightly with melted butter, and sprinkle lightly with sugar.

Bake for about 15 minutes.

Remove from oven and cool for 5 minutes before removing from cookie sheet.

FOR STRAWBERRIES:

1½ to 2 cups sliced strawberries

To prepare strawberries:

Combine sliced strawberries, sugar, and vanilla in a bowl. Set aside.

To build shortcake stacks:

Place 1 puff pastry round on a plate and spoon strawberries on top.

Put a second pastry round on top of that and add more strawberries.

Top with a third pastry round. Finish off with a dollop of whipped cream and 1 whole strawberry.

If your shortcake stack begins to slide, secure each pastry round to the next with a toothpick. Be careful not to bite the toothpicks.

Stack 'em high and eat 'em up!

1 tablespoon granulated sugar

½ teaspoon vanilla

FOR TOPPING:

Sweetened whipped cream

Strawberries for garnish

BLAST-OFF BLUEBERRY BISCUITS

Makes 8 servings

1 can large-size refrigerator biscuits

1 cup canned blueberry pie filling

¼ teaspoon ground nutmeg

¼ teaspoon almond extract

1 teaspoon ground cinnamon mixed with ¼ cup sugar

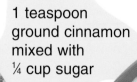

1. Preheat oven to 375 degrees.

2. Spray a 12-cup muffin pan with nonstick cooking spray. Divide each biscuit in half. Press half biscuit in bottom of 8 of the muffin cups, covering bottom completely. Leave 4 of the cups empty.

3. In a small bowl, combine blueberry pie filling, nutmeg, and almond extract.

4. Spoon 1 tablespoon of the blueberry pie filling on top of each biscuit half.

5. Cover the top of the blueberry filling with the other half of the biscuit.

6. Sprinkle each biscuit with a little of the cinnamon-sugar mixture.

7. Bake for about 15 minutes. Serve warm.

Blast off with an out-of-this-world flavor!

BONKERS FOR BANANA BREAD

Makes about 12 servings

3 ripe bananas

⅓ cup oil

1½ cups flour

¼ teaspoon salt

1 teaspoon baking powder

Preheat oven to 325 degrees.

Mash bananas in a mixing bowl.

Add remaining ingredients (except optional ingredients), stirring until just blended.

Fold in optional ingredients if you wish.

Pour into a greased 9 x 5-inch loaf pan or divide among 4 (4-inch) decorative baking pans.

Bake at 325 degrees for 1 hour for large pan or 25 to 30 minutes for smaller pans. Cool, then slice and serve.

Go bonkers!

½ cup sugar

1 egg

1 teaspoon vanilla

½ cup brown sugar

½ cup pecans, OR mini chocolate chips, OR dried cranberries (optional)

CAN YOU FONDUE?

¼ cup semisweet or milk chocolate chips

⅓ cup whipping cream

½ teaspoon vanilla

¼ cup white chocolate chips

Fruit (bananas, apples, pineapple, strawberries), washed and sliced or cut into bite-size pieces

Large marshmallows

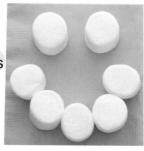

Pound cake or angel food cake, cut into bite-size pieces

Makes fondue for 4 to 6 people

1. Heat chocolate chips and cream in a microwave-safe dish for 1 minute. Stir and heat again for another 30 seconds.

2. Remove bowl from microwave and stir in vanilla. Transfer to a fondue pot, a 2-to-4-cup slow cooker, or a small decorative bowl.

3. Melt white chocolate chips for 30 seconds in microwave. Drizzle melted white chocolate on top of warm fondue.

4. Using fondue forks or wooden bamboo skewers, dip fruits, marshmallows, and pieces of cake into fondue.

Now you CAN fondue!

FRESH
FRUIT TARTS

Makes 12 tarts

1 package refrigerator piecrust dough

Flour for work surface

Purchased "hardening shell" chocolate ice cream topping OR vanilla yogurt

Fruit (grapes, strawberries, peaches, bananas, raspberries, pineapple, kiwi), washed and sliced or cut into bite-size pieces

1. Unfold 1 piecrust at a time and place on a lightly floured work surface.

2. Turn piecrust over to make sure both sides are lightly covered with flour. Gently roll out piecrust with rolling pin.

3. Using a 3-inch flower-shaped or round cookie cutter, carefully cut out pieces of piecrust. Place each cut-out crust in a 12-cup muffin pan that has been sprayed with nonstick cooking spray. Continue until both piecrusts are used.

4. Prick bottoms of each piecrust with a fork. Place prepared muffin pan in refrigerator for 30 minutes to chill.

5. Preheat oven to 350 degrees.

6. Remove muffin pan from refrigerator, and bake in oven for about 20 minutes or until crusts are golden brown. Remove from oven and cool 5 minutes.

7. Spread bottom of each tart shell with either the chocolate topping or a thin layer of vanilla yogurt. Arrange fruits of your choice on top, and chill in the refrigerator for 10 minutes or until ready to serve.

These fruit tarts are a sweet treat!

index